print
at the C O ▌

Print Room at the Coronet presents

As Good a Time As Any

by Peter Gill

As Good a Time As Any
received its world premiere at Print Room at the Coronet
on 30 April 2015

Supported using public funding by
**ARTS COUNCIL
ENGLAND**

LOTTERY FUNDED

As Good a Time As Any

by Peter Gill

Sylvia	**Lucy Fleming**
Marion	**Roberta Taylor**
Lily	**Tessa Bell-Briggs**
Gita	**Indira Joshi**
Shirley	**Olivia Llewellyn**
Bridget	**Eileen Pollock**
Amy	**Hayley Squires**
Joy	**Sharlene Whyte**

Director	**Peter Gill**
Designer	**Bruce McLean**
Lighting Designer	**Hartley T A Kemp**
Composer and Sound Designer	**Christian Mason**
Costume Supervisor	**Carrie Bayliss**
Casting Director	**Sarah Hughes**
Associate Director	**Max Key**
Assistant Designer	**Danielle Dent-Davis**
Production Electrician/ Assistant Lighting Designer	**Chris May**
Assistant to Bruce McLean	**Violet Vincent**
Scenic Painter	**Malcolm Key**
Hair	**Domenico Sansare** at Gina Conway
Musician: Flute	**Audrey Milherés**
Musician: Tuba	**Jack Adler-McKean**

Production Manager	**Andy Beardmore**
Stage Manager	**Hannah Gore**
Technical Stage Manager	**Charlotte Oliver**
Production thanks to:	**Philips Lighting**

Lucy Fleming (Sylvia)

Lucy first worked with Peter Gill in *A Collier's Friday Night* as part of the English Stage Company at the Royal Court. West End theatre credits include: *Richard II* and *Edward II* (Prospect and West End) *When Did You Last See My Mother*, *Out of the Question*, *Don't Start Without Me*, *Hay Fever*, *Middle-Age Spread*, *A Personal Affair*, *A Kind of Alaska*, *Our Song* and *The Constant Wife*. Other theatre credits include: *As You Like It*, *An Ideal Husband*, *A Patriot for Me*, *Time and the Conways* (all at Chichester Festival Theatre), *Twelfth Night* (Crucible Theatre), *A Yard of Sun* (Nottingham Playhouse). Also plays by Somerset Maugham, Rodney Acland, P G Wodehouse, Feydeau, Neil Simon, Christopher Fry and Harold Pinter.

Television credits include: *Richard II*, *Hay Fever*, *Smiley's People*, *Pride and Prejudice*, *Ever Decreasing Circles*, *The Avengers*, *Cold Warrior*, *Wycliffe*, *Nancherrow*, *A Dance to the Music of Time*, *Mr Bean*, *Heartbeat*, *Rosemary and Thyme*, *Law and Order* and *Survivors*.

Film credits include: Ken Loach's *A Misfortune*, *The Sorrows*, *Katherine Mansfield*, *The Boat that Rocked*.

Radio credits include: *Bond Correspondence*, *From Father with Love*, *Fifty Years of Chitty Chitty Bang Bang*.

As Producer: all fourteen of the James Bond novels.

Roberta Taylor (Marion)

Roberta was born in East London and trained at the Central School of Speech and Drama.

She began her professional career at the Citizens Theatre Glasgow, a theatre she has returned to many times in thirty-five years, most recently in 2014 to play Gertrude in *Hamlet*.

Other theatre credits include: *The Last of the DeMullins* and *The Reunion* (both at Jermyn Street), *Pygmalion* (Garrick), *The Entertainer*, *Winding the Ball* and *Arms and the Man* (all for Manchester Royal Exchange), *Romeo and Juliet* (Lyric), *A Free Country* (Tricycle), *The Seagull* (Birmingham Rep), *The Two Noble Kinsmen*, *The Lorencaccio Story* and *Sons of Light* (RSC).

Television credits include: series regulars for *The Bill* and *EastEnders*. Also *Holby City*, *Doctors*, *Father Brown*, *Bleak House*, *Silent Witness*, *The Knock*.

Film credits include: *The Witches*, *Tom and Viv*.

Roberta's other passion is writing and she has published two books so far: a memoir of her grandmother titled *Too Many Mothers*, which stayed in the *Sunday Times* top ten list for ten weeks, and a novel, *The Reinvention of Ivy Brown*. Last year, her letter to an unknown soldier was included in the published edition of the collection of letters. She is currently working on her third book.

Photo: Justin Canning

Tessa Bell-Briggs (Lily)

Tessa trained at the Rose Bruford College.

Her West End credits include: *Steaming* (Harold Pinter Theatre), *Situation Comedy* (Ambassadors Theatre) and *The Woman In Black* (Fortune Theatre). Tessa has played Anne-Marie in *A Doll's House* and Clara in *Hay Fever* (both for the Royal Exchange, Manchester) and Emily Brontë in *The Brontës of Haworth* (Stephen Joseph Theatre, directed by Alan Ayckbourn). Other work includes the title role in *Shirley Valentine* and Ange in *Abigail's Party*. Tessa has toured extensively in the UK and Germany and has played in repertory at the Churchill Theatre Bromley, the Nuffield Theatre, Southampton, the Library Theatre, Manchester, the Palace Theatre, Westcliff and the Century Theatre, Keswick.

Tessa's extensive television appearances include: *Poirot: The Third Girl* (Granada), *EastEnders*, *Holby City*, *Five Days*, *Harry Batt*, *The Grid*, *Silent Witness*, *Birds of a Feather*, *Play for Today* and *The Brittas Empire* (all for the BBC), a Russian con woman in *Skins* (Channel 4) and several characters in *The Bill* and *Rumpole of the Bailey* (Thames).

Tessa recently filmed the feature *The Christmas Candle* with Susan Boyle (Pinewood Films).

Indira Joshi (Gita)

Indira's recent television credits include: Amrita in *Vera* (ITV), Deepa in *Toast* (Channel 4), Mrs Khan in *Frankie* (BBC), Grishma in *Coronation Street* (ITV), Erin in *Red Dwarf* (BBC), Pushpa Bakshi in *Indian Doctor* (Rondo Productions), Chilha's Mother in *Life is Not All Ha Ha He Hee* (BBC), and Madhuri in *The Kumars at Number 42*, Series 1–7.

Recent film includes: Kamala in *Blue Tower* (Raindance Award).

Theatre work in Delhi includes a host of plays by dramatists such as Lorca, Molière and Stoppard.

Recent UK theatre includes: Itbar's Mother in *Dara* and Lady Woodvill in *The Man of Mode* (National Theatre), Renu in *One Night* (Theatre Royal Stratford East) and Khalda in *Balti Kings* (Tamasha).

As well as her extensive acting career, Indira has worked in voice-over and presenting. She DJ'd on radio *A Date With You* in Delhi, and edited the award-winning *New World Times* in San Francisco.

Olivia Llewellyn (Shirley)

Olivia trained at Lamda.

Theatre includes: *Les Liaisons Dangereuses* (West End), *Comedy of Errors* (RSC), *Shell Seekers* (UK tour), *For Services Rendered* (The Watermill), *Timon of Athens* (National Theatre).

Television includes: *Passer By, Doctors, Midsomer Murders, The Genius of Beethoven, Kingdom, Lucan, Penny Dreadful* seasons 1–2, *Musketeers, Call the Midwife, The Lizzie Borden Chronicles.*

Film credits include: *Dimensions, The Death of Merlin, The Boat that Rocked.*

Eileen Pollock (Bridget)

Since co-founding the women's theatre groups Bloomers and Camouflage, Eileen has worked with most major Irish theatres (both touring and in-house), and taken theatre roles in Britain including Miss Hannigan in *Annie*, Masha in *Three Sisters*, Brecht's *Mother Courage*, and various other roles from Shakespeare to panto. She was also the first Anna in Marie Jones' *Women on the Verge of HRT*. Recently she has played Mag in *Beauty Queen of Leenane*, The Murderess in Rona Munro's *Iron*, the Irish-American labour activist Mother Jones, and Kathleen Behan of Dublin's infamous Behan family, both in ongoing one-woman shows. She currently works internationally with Global Arts Corps on a Northern Irish project about people coming out of recent conflict situations.

On film she has worked with Ron Howard, Mike Leigh and Sydney McCartney. Eileen was Lilo Lil in the BBC's long-running sitcom *Bread*.

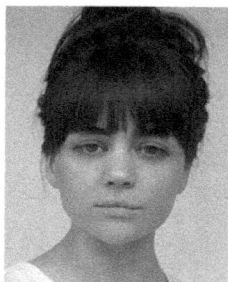

Hayley Squires (Amy)

Hayley trained at Rose Bruford College and graduated in 2010.

Television credits include: *Southcliffe, Murder ep1, Complicit* and *Call the Midwife*.

Film credits include: *Polar Bear, A Royal Night Out, Blood Cells* and *Away*.

Her writing credits include: *Vera Vera Vera* (Upstairs at the Royal Court), *Glitterland* (Lyric Hammersmith), *Educator* (BBC Radio 3), *Blue Glory* (BBC Radio 4).

She is currently under commision with the Gate Theatre and the Royal Court Theatre.

Sharlene Whyte, (Joy)

Sharlene trained at RADA.

Theatre credits include: *Nut* (National Theatre), *Treasure Island* (Theatre Royal Haymarket), *Julius Caesar* (Lyric Hammersmith), *Compact Failure* (Arcola Theatre), *Born Bad* (Hampstead Theatre), *The Three Birds* (Gate Theatre), *Arabian Night* (Young Vic), *Guiding Light* (Nottingham).

Television credits include: *Critical, Jonathan Creek, Savant's Thumb, Sadie J, Truckers, Run, Mightier than the Sword, Spooks, Coronation Street, Doctors, Waterloo Road, Silent Witness, Casualty, Tracey Beaker, Tinsel Town, As If.*

Film credits include: *Second Coming, High Heels and Low Lifes, Second Nature.*

Peter Gill

Peter Gill was born in 1939 in Cardiff and started his professional career as an actor. A director as well as a writer, he has directed over a hundred productions in the UK, Europe and North America, and is the founding director of Riverside Studios and the Royal National Theatre Studio. At the Royal Court Theatre in the 1960s, he was responsible for introducing D. H. Lawrence's plays to the theatre. His plays include *The Sleepers Den* (Royal Court, London, 1965), *Over Gardens Out* (Royal Court, London, 1968), *Small Change* (Royal Court, London, 1976), *Kick for Touch* (National Theatre, London, 1983), *Cardiff East* (National Theatre, London, 1997), *Certain Young Men* (Almeida Theatre, 1999), *The York Realist* (English Touring Theatre, 2001), *Original Sin* (Sheffield Crucible, 2002), *Another Door Closed* (Theatre Royal, Bath, 2009) and *A Provincial Life* (National Theatre of Wales, Sherman Cymru, Cardiff, 2011), *Versailles* (Donmar Warehouse, 2014). His plays are published by Faber and Faber.

Bruce McLean (Designer)

Bruce McLean is a Scottish sculptor and painter. He studied at Glasgow School of Art, and at St Martin's School of Art, where he studied with Anthony Caro and Phillip King. In reaction to what he regarded as the academicism of his teachers he began making sculpture from rubbish. McLean has gained international recognition for his paintings, ceramics, prints, work with film, theatre and books. McLean was Head of Graduate Painting at the Slade School of Fine Art, London. He has had numerous one-man exhibitions including at the Tate Gallery, the Modern Art Gallery in Vienna and the Museum of Modern Art, Oxford.

Hartley T A Kemp (Lighting Designer)

Hartley is from London and is now based in the UK and Australia. Work with Peter Gill incudes *Certain Young Men*, *Days of Wine and Roses*, *Original Sin*, *Romeo and Juliet*, *Scenes from the Big Picture*, *The Voysey Inheritance*, *The York Realist*. His London work includes West End, National, RSC, Donmar, Old Vic, Royal Court, Almeida, BAC, Bush, Gate, Hampstead, Lyric Hammersmith, Theatre503, Tricycle, Menier Chocolate Factory, ROH Linbury, Southwark Playhouse, Stratford East. UK regional work includes Birmingham Rep, Bristol Old Vic, Clwyd Teatr Cymru, Exeter Northcott, Manchester Royal Exchange, Sheffield Theatres, West Yorkshire Playhouse, English Touring Theatre, Paines Plough. Work in Europe includes Gate, Dublin; English Theatre, Frankfurt; Gothenburg Opera; Tiroler Landesteater, Innsbruck. In South Africa: Fugard, Cape Town. In US: Broadway, Off-Broadway, Regional. Australia includes Sydney Theatre Company, Belvoir, Griffin Theatre Company; Melbourne Theatre Company, Malthouse; Siren Theatre, Ride On Theatre. Hartley is artistic director of C venues at the Edinburgh Festival Fringe.

Christian Mason (Composer and Sound Designer)

A 2015 winner of an Ernst von Siemens Musikstiftung Composer Prize, Christian Mason is enjoying a prolific career with an array of forthcoming commissions including a piece for Pierre Boulez's ninetieth birthday to be performed at the Lucerne Festival, a work to be recorded by Klangforum Wien, a composition for the Radio-France programme, *Alla Breve*, and another for the opening of the Asian Arts Theatre in Gwangju, Korea in 2016, a project curated by Unsuk Chin. Christian's works have been previously performed at, among others, the Lucerne Festival, Tanglewood Festival of Contemporary Music and Spitalfields Festival by musicians such as Jean-Guihen Queyras, James MacMillan, London Sinfonietta, London Symphony Orchestra, and BBC Philharmonic.

Max Key (Associate Director)

Max Key trained on the National Theatre Directors' Course and works in theatre, film and opera.

Directing credits include: *Year 10* (Finborough Theatre – *Time Out* Critics' Choice Award), *Mariana Pineda* (Arcola Theatre), *Wilde Tales* (Southwark Playhouse), *Up the Royal Borough* (Lyric Hammersmith), *The Turn of the Screw* and *The Rape of Lucretia* (Arcola Theatre). Short film: *Preservation* (Palm Springs and BAFTA).

Assistant directing credits include: *The Flying Dutchman* (Royal Opera House), *The Voysey Inheritance* (National Theatre) and *La Bohème* (Royal Albert Hall).

Max has taught and directed extensively at leading drama schools including Guildhall, LAMDA and Mountview. Credits include: *Cymbeline*, *The Way of the World*, *Summerfolk*, *August Osage County* and *Jerusalem*.

www.maxkey.co.uk

print room
at *the* CORONET

The Print Room was founded in 2010 by Artistic Director Anda Winters in a converted printing workshop in Notting Hill. Over the last five years, the intimate West London theatre has built a reputation for producing and curating a highly acclaimed and varied programme of performance and visual arts, including theatre, dance, music, exhibitions and multidisciplinary collaborations, in a friendly and welcoming environment.

Recent highlights include the UK premieres of Howard Barker's *Lot and His God* and Jon Fosse's *The Dead Dogs*, the world premieres of new contemporary dance commissions FLOW (set in water) and IGNIS (inspired by fire), the major revivals of Brian Friel's *Molly Sweeney* and Will Eno's *Thom Pain (Based on Nothing)*, experimental art/opera *Triptych*, live-art performance *Alice Anderson's Travelling Factory*, as well as the re-imagination of modern classics such as Harold Pinter's *The Dumb Waiter*, Arthur Miller's *The Last Yankee* and the award-winning production of *Uncle Vanya*.

When developers took over the original Print Room building in 2014, the charity moved to its new permanent home, Notting Hill's The Coronet, where it opened its doors for the company's inaugural autumn season in October 2014 to present the first theatrical performance in The Coronet for nearly a century.

The Coronet began life as a Victorian playhouse back in 1898 and later became a legendary cinema. The Print Room will restore the iconic venue in stages, to take the space back to its theatrical roots while improving its cinema facilities.

Over the next three years, the Print Room's ambitions will expand as the main auditorium is reopened, alongside the flexible studio theatre, to bring world-class cinema on 35mm and new digital facilities to its audience.

This will allow the building to offer cross-arts programming between the two major spaces while continuing to create work with emerging and established artists from all fields.

For Print Room at the Coronet

**The Print Room is a privately funded charity
that receives no regular public subsidy.**

We are dependent on the generosity of our supporters to present our work.
Thank you to all the supporters, colleagues and friends who have helped us
on our journey so far. We would not be here without their kind support.

The Print Room is generously supported by

Corporate Sponsors

markit   **Studio Indigo Ltd**
ARCHITECTS & INTERIOR DESIGNERS   AUTONOMOUS

Markit are match-funders and supporters
of the Print Room outreach ticket scheme.

HEADLINE
Allen Fisher Foundation, Clive & Helena Butler,
Paulo & Aud Cuniberti, Mike Fisher,
Roderick & Elizabeth Jack, Amanda Waggott

CAPITAL
Anon, Ben & Louisa Brown, Glenda Burkhart, Matt Cooper,
John & Jennifer Crompton, Ayelet Elstein, Lara Fares, Connie Freeman,
Ashish Goyal, Tom & Maarit Glocer, Julian Granville & Louisiana Lush,
Debbie Hannam, Anne Herd, Angela Massey, Posgate Charitable Trust,
The Ruddock Foundation for the Arts, Alison Winter

BOLD
John & Laura Banes, Bill Reeves & Debbie Berger, Tony & Kate Best,
Bruno & Christiane Boesch, Caroline & Ian Cormack, Victoria Gray,
Cecile Guillon, Isabelle Hotimsky, Martin Jacomb, Kristen Kennish,
Amy Lashinsky, David Leathers, Jonathan Levy, Tony Mackintosh,
Matt & Amanda McEvoy, Julia Rochester, Lois Sieff, Rita Skinner,
Antony Thomlinson, Vahiria Vedet Janbon, Pamela Williams

Special thanks to
Aki Ando, Mimi Gilligan, Louisa Lane Fox

Peter Gill

Peter Gill was born in 1939 in Cardiff and started his
professional career as an actor. A director as well as a
writer, he has directed over a hundred productions in the
UK, Europe and North America. At the Royal Court
Theatre in the sixties, he was responsible for introducing
D. H. Lawrence's plays to the theatre. The founding
director of Riverside Studios and the Royal National
Theatre Studio, Peter Gill lives in London. His plays
include *The Sleepers Den* (Royal Court, London, 1965),
A Provincial Life (Royal Court, 1966), *Over Gardens
Out* (Royal Court, 1968), *Small Change* (Royal Court,
1976), *Kick for Touch* (National Theatre, London, 1983),
Cardiff East (National Theatre, 1997), *Certain Young
Men* (Almeida Theatre, London, 1999), *The York Realist*
(English Touring Theatre, 2001), *Original Sin* (Sheffield
Crucible, 2002), *Another Door Closed* (Theatre Royal,
Bath, 2009), *A Provincial Life* (National Theatre of
Wales, Sherman Cymru, Cardiff, 2011) and *Versailles*
(Donmar Warehouse, London, 2014).

PETER GILL

As Good a Time As Any

ff

FABER & FABER

First published in 2015
by Faber and Faber Limited
74–77 Great Russell Street, London WC1B 3DA

Typeset by Country Setting, Kingsdown, Kent CT14 8ES
Printed and bound by CPI Group (UK) Ltd, Croydon, CR0 4YY

A CIP record for this book is available
from the British Library

978-0-571-32642-6

2 4 6 8 10 9 7 5 3 1

As Good a Time As Any was first produced by Print Room at the Coronet, London, on 30 April 2015. The cast was as follows:

Sylvia Lucy Fleming
Marion Roberta Taylor
Lily Tessa Bell Briggs
Shirley Olivia Llewellyn
Bridget Eileen Pollock
Amy Hayley Squires
Gita Indira Joshi
Joy Sharlene Whyte

Director Peter Gill
Designer Bruce McLean
Lighting Designer Hartley T. A. Kemp
Composer and Sound Designer Christian Mason
Costume Supervisor Carrie Bayliss
Associate Director Max Key

Characters

Sylvia

Marion

Lily

Shirley

Bridget

Amy

Gita

Joy

AS GOOD A TIME AS ANY

Chorus One

Sylvia, Marion, Lily, Shirley, Bridget, Amy, Gita, Joy

Sylvia
why was i up so early   you always have to wait   as
if getting up early will ensure you are on time   which i
wasn't in the end   and Ronnie up not long after   me
into the garden before i dressed   and it was quite cold
i was surprised at how   i hope Kevin will come this
week   but then i had left it with him   why do I still
think there will be a post early   the daffodils all gone
the tulips still to come   i thought to hear from Hilda
i suppose she will ring   i hope she will ring   not that
it makes a difference   Ronnie will be there   i have
today and tomorrow in my diary   with a question
mark   useless to hope for a letter from Catherine
she'll email her father   Roger rang   and Ronnie out
to get the *Telegraph*   he's having trouble again with his
tenant in the top flat   Ronnie had some breakfast   i
just had tea   and left a note for Imelda to make up the
bed in the small bedroom for Hilda   she used to drive
herself up and stay at her club when she came to town
but now comes on the train   though she could park
here   but too old now to drive on a motorway i
suppose   not that you'd think it   and she's no bother
he was up on the roof again   and Roger not insured
for it   and i like to see her   and reminds me of
Mummy   says things like i'm a getting a tum   i feel
as if i had a lot to do and i haven't really   but i've got
to think about what to wear next week   i was hoping
we didn't have to go this year   but Ronnie wants to
so i mustn't be mean   i was hoping to hear from

Catherine   about when to expect her next week   i
can hear her saying oh Mummy   but there we are
Hilda's not much in town now   she comes now to see
her solicitor   who looks after her money   Mummy
used to say i think i'll go down and see Hilda   and
you'd think they had nothing in common   Roger's
tenant had been out on the flat roof on the top of the
house again   and he'd be liable   and he drinks
nothing from Jeremy either   and i shan't ring again
until he does   and she makes me feel i must watch my
tongue   i'm going to say the wrong thing as far as the
children are concerned   and i do think she's too
controlling with them   anyway we hardly see them
lately   and i know how much this is all due to her
and i'm so proud of him   so i mustn't fuss   but i
always feel we're rationed   but then i have a feeling
she's like that with her mother too   and she asked if
they can come for some of half term   so that'll be nice
and Ronnie will like that   i hope Imelda will make the
bed up   i'm sure she will   but i miss Maria   i asked
Imelda if she saw her   they go to the same church
and how she was doing   she's living in   she's better
off   if only one had the money   and might be
cheaper   well Mother when she was first married did
and granny did   and my other Granny had a
housekeeper and chauffeur   just Mrs Saunders and a
daily   when we knew her   and the man to do the
garden   i shouldn't think it since Imelda is fine   but
with Maria i never had to think   she's asked me to give
money for a school needing funds   i left some and
sealed it in a little printed envelope she left for me   to
show it's above board   they are so good at collecting
must be such a comfort   she has two of her children
somewhere in the middle east   strange for both us to
have children there   and i had shopping to do   and
in the end rushed

Marion

Tina said she'd walk the dog to give me more time to get
myself ready   but she didn't come for an age   I was
up and out before she came   she had to bring the little
one   when he said he'd take him to his mother's on his
way to work   but he had to go out early she said
she won't hear of me criticising him   cuts me off if i
say anything about him   and she had to take the other
two to school on top of it   he knew she was coming to
me   it's like this whenever she does anything for me
lately   and he plays on as if he's doing her a favour
his mother thinks the sun shines   and half the time he
acts if he was single   thinks after he's provided the
money he's on his own   and i still can't forget the other
thing   still that's over   thank God   and he took
them on   and he treats the big one as his own   i hope
John comes later   i want him to look at my washing
machine   anyway i'll l have the little one tomorrow
it's too much for her   and i said so   even if it is a
part-time job   i asked John about this girl he's been
seeing   why do you want to know he said   i said i'm
interested   stay interested he said   and he talks of
starting a business and going into property and giving up
his trade   where have i heard talk like that   Joanne
is the only sensible one   she said she'll be over the
weekend   and the little one is out of hospital   she's a
child in a million that one   so that that's it   for the
time being   thank God   that woman lost her dog
she still goes for a walk at the same time   morning and
afternoon   but no reason for it   i said are you going
to get another   i don't know if I'd get another now
saw the man with the boxer when i was out   too big
for London i think   but such a lovely dog   i let him
have a run on his own when we get back   he barks to
come in when he's ready   this morning the man who
has moved in next door but one not long rang the bell

said he knew he was mine   and thought he was loose
and Tina says you know what Mum   chance would be
a fine thing   she says her father has threatened to get
a dog   and i just know what he'd get   wouldn't he
love it   he's another one who can't grow up   oh well
he won't keep it of course   at least that's one thing i
don't have to worry about   let him do what he wants
John'll come in later I hope   and i need him to look at
the light in the hall

Sylvia
i took a short cut again through the cemetery in the end
if it is a short cut   having got up early thought I would
be late   i had to get some shopping for dinner   Hilda
will have lunch in town   i should have thought   she'll
come up early i think and leave her bag   i went to the
patisserie to get some of those little custard tarts   and
then to the Polish tailor   took Ronnie's trousers   i
can't wear that dress again   it's marked terribly   and
i can't hide it with anything   so there's that   and i
don't want to go   and came this way through the
cemetery   i don't know how much of a short cut it is
it's so peaceful   full of blossom   like big white
umbrellas   and bluebells touching on the graves
such a lot of thought   i'm very impressed by the
upkeep   and it's only borough cemetery   this
morning pale blue   creamy pale blue   bride's mother
blue   powder   no paler blue   and   paler sky
shining through   with one mass of dark cloud sheered
up like an awning   i went to look at the big magnolia
and the forsythia   where there is a soldier's grave
under it in the shade   there are soldiers' graves
scattered throughout   mostly from the great war
some few from the second war more organised   in a
little graveyard of their own   they seem to let the grass
do what it likes in some places   so in the summer it's

left high   i don't look when i walk on the path near the
children's graves   i can't look for more than a glance
at the little dolls and toys and windmills among the
artificial flowers   there would be no meaning would
there   how would you survive it   makes me think it
was bad enough for me with Jeremy   and i think thank
God it was only that with J   it doesn't seem so bad
and i'm so proud of him   and i touch wood   touch
anything   Philippa rang me again last night   to talk
about John Ashton   and i really i didn't want to
there were more obits in the papers yesterday   and a
picture   so that was a shock   and started all kinds of
thinking   and Pippa wanting to talk about it   the
Polish woman must be a catholic too   there was
picture of the virgin stuck on the wall

Lily

i was waiting dressed and waiting for ages   until i
thought they weren't coming   do you think i'd forget
you he said   and it's a lovely morning in spite of how
i felt   for i didn't feel up to it   and i've always been
fine first thing   but you know i felt sick and fed up
again   and what's the use of it   but it's been lovely
morning   lovely spring morning lovely i must say
but got the proper blues   feeling so weak   and not
up to it   even to go into the garden   and it's not like
me   dear dear   and then when they came   because
i'd been waiting like a lemon   i was a bit short with
him   and it wasn't his fault   and he's not the least bit
familiar   but he's nice   and just as we was leaving
the young woman come to do my shopping   i'd prefer
to go myself   but i can't on days like this   but you
feel you can't be picky   and tell them   and yet they
never get it   what i want   exactly   and i'm too
particular   and i couldn't place my spare key to give to
her   i must find it   she'll leave the shopping in the

porch   it'll be safe   time was could have left it with
Mrs Hancock   when she was here   and while i was
waiting i saw her son going to the woman housebound
on the corner   every day he comes   sometimes twice
a day   can't have much of a life   and does her garden
and never smiles   a big car there too sometimes
that's not him i think   another son   i wish i could
do more in my garden   but i haven't got the energy
yesterday i tried   and i couldn't manage   but at least
it's brighter this last week   and that cheers you   i
don't mind the cold so much   if it's bright   but all
the dark days went on and on   but different when it's a
bright spring day   like today the sky blue when i went
out   blue as blue   and my tulips will be out   i put
some in the same time as the daffs   all the crocuses are
out   the snowdrops long gone   everything seems
gone before they've even bloomed   such is the time
slipping   and the wallflowers are in   i don't know
that bluebells suit a garden   where did they come from
i never put them there did i at home there was a wood
beyond the village   and we fancied if you lay among
them you would fall asleep   how did they get there
bluebells   they don't seem natural to me in a garden
her garden needs looking at   i cut back her hydrangea
just before she went   i miss our coffee in the morning
i thought I'd have heard from her by now   she said
she'd keep in touch   but false as fire   he said   the
young man   you seemed surprised that i come for you
you thought i'd forget you   he's such a nice boy   and
i was grateful   thought of him of course   of them
first thing   and thinking of both of them   when i was
sat there waiting

Shirley
up early as if that would ameliorate the waiting   dread
of course first thing and lie under it with your chest

tightening   when at night let it float up   and all
parked there safe   and feel the blessedness of there
being nothing more   knowing that sleeping in will
make it worse   all the anxieties reassembled   when at
night you are free   except for the dreams   if they
come   but all the fears reassembling themselves   as
you lie there waiting   i bathed last night like a child
so as to be ready   and washed my hair   and ironed
this   so as to be the more ready   i was up as soon as
it was light   and into the bathroom and dressed   and
lay on the sofa at first   listening for the birds in the
dark under the quilt   and waiting for the light   and
drifting into a doze   and the birds singing while it was
still dark   and waiting for a blackbird that is so sweet
amongst all the tweeting is it   and listen to the radio
then up when it was bright into the kitchen   and did
some washing-up that was left   as if doing things will
be the end of it somehow   not relief for a time   not
the comfort in the doing   but feel that if i do this   as
i am doing it   will be the end this time   and i had
time to do some work   but too unsettled   why do i
feel that i have gone back   that this has taken me back
that i am feeling as i used to   but Graham is there
and Dad   it's Dad's birthday this month   and thought
of him   is that it   and i was out of the front door
feeling like Jane Grey stumbling towards the block

Lily
and i am not usually one for worry   and i knew they
would come for me   but couldn't be certain what the
arrangement was   and so was all of a fidget and
uncertainty   and the little one came to mind   as i was
waiting of course   not a day goes by but he comes to
mind   my dear little one   sometimes i have to be
strong   and put them out of my mind   both of them
for you have to be strong and get on with things   and

not live thinking all the time of the past   but how i like
to think of them   and it's worth the sadness   for it is
a comfort as well to think of them   how i wished he
was here this morning   to see his lovely face   oh i did
wish it   but the young man was so kind   so that
cheered me up   he cheered me up   but increasingly
i wonder I am still here

Bridget
i had to walk past again this morning   it's the only
way   unless i want to go round the houses   but i
didn't have the time   i can usually avoid it   but even
when i'm going to Mary's   i still go the long way round
i wish I could get more sense   there were men as usual
outside waiting for their sandwiches   only three of
them today   two of them you'd expect   an old fellow
i've seen in the mall   and a big young fellow   leaning
against the wall so as not to be remarked on   and a
middle-aged man you wouldn't have expected to see there
i couldn't see clearly who it was opened the door to
hand the packages out   i think it was the one i see
going into Marks and Spencer shopping   not anyone
from my time   how would there be   but they gave
me a job   when i was in strange country   with just a
letter in my hand   and fair do's in their way good to
me   and what else would i have done i was so young
and Bernie who i came over with had gone back home
and it was a godsend really   and when i fell pregnant
they were good to me they tried to persuade me to give
her up   for her sake they said   as much as for my
sake   but now thanks be to God I had the strength
and they meant well   but i don't want to think of
those times   childish   but they come to mind   the
two of them do at any rate   the superior and the one
who had the management of it   she had a streak of
disappointments   and a temper on her   ooh yes

and the sulks on her   the superior was sunny   was
more untroubled   sunny and plump   but not so
savvy   she was so innocent   oh so not of the world
the other you felt belonged in the world if she was being
true   and the disappointment was there   i thank God
it's in the past   and they found me a position
looking after the old skinflint who was thick with the
priest there   and i went and worked for him   and the
old skinflint left all the cash to the church and his old
cousin he saw once in a blue moon when she was
visiting   and nothing between them   after the years
i spent cleaning up after him   but it gave me time with
the baby   and i had a flat of my own before long
through the council by then   but he was an old villain
from the dark ages bitter old twister he was   and why
am i saying that now   and i don't like to think of all
that even for all they did   for i haven't kept up my
faith   and glad to be out of it all

Marion

i told her to tell her father I saw Danny Pursey on Friday
when he was going in to put a bet on   when i was up
the market   he've come back to live over here again
he was looking very poorly   very thin   only his eyes
had anything of the Danny i knew   looking done in
none of his gypsy look   with a younger woman
rough as you can get   and shuffling in to the betting shop
like an old man   oh Danny dear   broke my heart
broke many a heart Danny   then he's been married
twice   if he was married the second time   i don't
know how many kids   he looked so ill   i said you
looking after yourself   you're not looking after yourself
and he was pleased to see me   hello Marion   but
then he was always a lovely boy   so soft   and his
lovely face   and he was pleased to see me   i think he
was looking worse than if he was on the booze and the

drugs   anyway he looked terrible   and that put the
kybosh on it then   and i cried bitter when i got home
i was feeling sorry for myself anyway   but seeing him
oh dear

Amy
he didn't come back on Tuesday night either   so i went
round his friend's yesterday   to see if he was there
but he'd gone to his mother's   and i don't want to go
up there   i've rung him on his mobile and texted him
but he never replies to messages   he don't want to
know he says   he's not up to it he says   and she said
good riddance when i called in there on the way this
morning   she's always up early now   says she don't
sleep   i was up early with the baby   don't accept
crumbs   you've been accepting crumbs   he's not
worth it she said   but that's easy for her to say   oh
i wish he'd come back   he's not up to it he says   but i
wish he'd come back   this is a pain in my heart   she
said she'd have the baby for the morning   but i said i
don't know how long i'll be   i'll go in on my way
home   and i'll take something for tea   and then
perhaps   i'll go round Donna's   but that won't do
that's not fair   no no   i always think it's me   all
of it   i always think it's my fault   it's not your fault
you was doing well   you want to forget him   and don't
have him back   you was like this before   don't have
him back   you got to think about yourself and baby
you got a lot on your plate now as well   but i love
him   i do   she asked me if i wanted to stop round
hers for a couple of nights   but i must stick it
out   she's on her own now   the old man been dead
eighteen months now   she said you're the only one i
see now   i said you see Paul   who she had for a
while before me   and Linda   but she lives miles away
now she said   and she's not seen her for ages she said

i haven't seen Paul for months either   he's been
working hard she said   so he's alright   he's caught up
with this girl she said   anyway I'll go round there for
tea later   i'll have to see to the baby in minute   see
he needs a drink

Shirley
i walked to the café   and sat outside in the sunlight
under the plane tree   drinking my coffee   and feeling
better in the warm   and feeling how much better things
have been   until this pulling me back   so in spite of it
things are better than the stasis   the waiting for a life
i have crossed a line invisible to the people   so in spite
of it now   i can still take in   now   last week   the
light like smoke through the drizzle   and take in this
lovely day   and the blueness in the sky   the silver
balloon caught up in the tree   and the chair on the
river bed   without it overwhelming me   or becoming
a mirror for the look on a child's face   the furrow on
its little brow   the frown as it sits faced with a decision
being made for it   going to school   or in a hospital
bed   or on a television programme   it's better to be
noticing the thickness of the camellias without worry
no longer waiting for a life   stuck in Mum's unhappiness
and the mess of my finals   this is better even as it is
today   waiting here   it is better than life then   than
standing by the filing cabinet   stirring coffee in a cup
sitting with my coffee and my lunch   my apple from
my desk drawer   standing with my coffee   wearing a
dark green sweater   wearing my dark green sweater
a dark green polo neck   i can see myself slowly stirring
the coffee in the cup   the coffee didn't mix   the water
didn't boil   hoping then that everything bad has
already happened   and then coming to the conclusion
to leave   and take life outside Marchmont Street
and the library   even this is better than that   stuck in

Mum's unhappiness   and Graham is there this week
always my adjacence   but i have crossed a line

Sylvia
why didn't i ring her Hilda   if i was so concerned
still she'd think i was fussing and might have rung
i could have rung   but i was out so early   perhaps
i'll ring Catherine later   and i never get the time right
and when i get home i'll find she has rung anyway
Hilda has rung i am sure   why didn't i fix a time
and what does it matter   really Mummy she'd say
i'm sure it will be fine   thank God that she's safe   but
how can you be certain   she's more adventurous than
me   than I could ever have been   i might pop into
Roger   on my on my way home   if i've got the
energy   he'll have to bring things to a head   and i
have letters to write   and the bills   my grandmother
used to do her correspondence every morning in bed
he was moaning about his tenant's drinking without
doing anything about it   and he thinks it will come out
alright   without raising a finger   always relying on
his charm   and dodging the issue   he's not straight
with his woman friend either   he'll never give her what
she wants   and he thinks because he's honest with her
about what he can commit to   that lets him off the
hook   and poor little thing's expecting more i can tell
and she looks so disappointed   with a sallow little face
poor woman   he shouldn't keep her in hope   men
have the upper hand in these things

Gita
he was already doing the papers when i got up   they
were all still sleeping   i was so anxious when i got out
of bed   so i showered and then puja   said my prayers
and felt better for it   then the baby woke them and i
made the breakfast   while she saw to the baby   and
he and Rhajiv did the papers   and then i had the baby

i didn't know what to wear   he said he would come
with me   as if we could leave just her on her own with
a baby now   Rhajiv said he'd take me on his way to
work   but too far out of his way   Shilpa would have
come with me if i'd asked her   so it's my fault   though
i think she could have offered   and she rang me before
i left   and she's got her studying   and that boy she's
caught up with   i wish she was still at home   but then
but she says there's not enough room   and where would
she work   and of course i worry about her   he's got
to go to the cash and carry anyway today   don't worry
don't worry   Indira said i should wear my Punjab suit
i took two buses   only two buses and not crowded
and there's stock in out the back only half checked   i'll
get a minicab home   or i'll ring him and he will pick
me up   or Rhajiv will pick me up   i could have asked
Shilpa   she offered   i wish i had for she's always a
comfort to me   so i worry will he check   will he
check   will you check   and Indira's a good girl   but
she will do it her own way   so i don't know what she'll
be cooking tonight   i left it to her   but who knows
what she'll do   anyway   and while i'm down here
i could get some shopping

Joy

he usually comes to me today   she brings him about
eleven   then after lunch she can go to her meeting at
the church   so she'll have to miss it again today   and
she won't think of anyone else having him   and there's
no thought of Garry having him   well she'd never
think of it   and nor would he   even though he loves
him and spoils him   and she won't think of the future
even for a short time   and i am sure there is a place for
him to go to for her to have a break   and he'd like it
he's so good natured   and then eventually   though i
don't want to think about it

Amy

i didn't tell her I'd seen my mum the weekend   she
don't mind   but she says i always upset myself   and
she wasn't so bad this time   better than last time   last
time i saw her   last time i went   she was in a right
mess   she couldn't manage at all   every time she tries
to get herself together   it don't last more than a couple
of months   and she's said enough times she's sorry
enough times   and i think there's nothing she can do
but she wasn't so bad this time   but this feeling   oo
even when she gets straightened out it don't last   no use
blaming is it   and i didn't tell her when I went round
this morning   but if i do tell her she says she understands
but she thinks i always upset myself   she says it's my
business   and i have to do it   i have to see her   so i
haven't told her   i don't want to go on about everything
and she said   how come you met that little villain
she's says you're kidding yourself   this is too hard
it's all too hard   i can't think what i'll do   if he don't
come back

Bridget

why i'm thinking so much about that then now   i don't
know   i can't put it out of my mind   they say he used
to collect for the boys   but then there was a lot of that
here then   Mary says they collected in the pub near me
you wouldn't think so if you went in there now
according to Mary   the landlord went round quietly
after calling time   and the old man   he was in with
the council in those days too   which did his business
no harm   who am I to judge   it's none of my
business   but still he was terrible old hypocrite
anyway   and it's all in the past   and i haven't been to
church not for years   and yet i feel i should go to
church   and i'll never have any luck   and i still say
my prayers sometimes   for the children i do   and it
would be a comfort   but i can't believe all that's said

Joy

and he'd be used to it   so she could have peace   but
she won't discuss it   it's in God's hands she says   and
so it goes on being avoided   and I don't know how to
bring it to a head   she tries to change the subject   if
i do try to talk about it   and it's not worth it   she
makes me guilty   and i feel bad for thinking about it
and it's hard even to think about it for long   and not
solving it   and i have children of my own   and then
i feel terrible   and i think i'll manage   and then i put
everything away   and we go week to week   and I
don't mind   i could say God will look after him
meaning me after she's gone   and i feel bad for saying
it   she just assumes it   and doesn't want to talk
about it   and i want him to get used to care now   she
knows i wouldn't abandon him   I love him   she's
afraid they'll take him from her she says   as if they
would   and then i feel for her

Bridget

Mary is going to come to find me if she finishes her shift
early   she wants to go to bingo   but i don't think i'll
be up to it   Clare says she'll come on Saturday   she'll
bring the little one   the big ones won't come now   he
used to love his nan   but he plays football   and she
goes to her dancing   they don't want their nan so
much now   but i'll go up there for a week later   and
that'll be nice   and then i can pet the baby   and he'll
be grown before we know it   i wish they were still here
but you can't have everything   and i'll take him to the
park   and we'll go shopping on Saturday   Mary says
you're lucky not to have them always saying Mum can
you have him   i wouldn't mind   i miss them   i do
but still it's a good chance for them this job   and he's
good as gold   and he's not close to his family   and
it's not all that far   and there's Declan's golden wedding

will i go over   the girl rang me   oo   i suppose i
should   but i've never liked her   but nice of them to
ask me   i haven't seen them for an age   and perhaps
she'll come with me   if i can find the money

Joy
and i had a time with him this morning   he's giving up
his football   and he's been playing about in school
they put him with some very nice man last time   who
talked him out of it   when he was bunking off   thank
God she's as good as gold and no bother   i'm blessed
with her for sure   anyway tonight it'll take me out of
myself   i hope   Garry is coming too this evening
and he's bringing the big one   then he'll look after the
kids for me

Marion
and by coincidence i saw Rita Eady   the day before
i seen Danny   who i haven't seen for an age   and
she said she seen Georgie Wyle   who come up from
Kent to see his mother   i said to tell her father   he
and Danny fancied themselves   didn't they though
and Georgie didn't say boo to a goose was the one went
and joined a band and had a record deal   he's still
married   lives in Ironbridge   i said tell your father
i seen them

Sylvia
Mummy would have known what to do   and Mimi
certainly would   but then she would have something
else to wear   both of them would   or they would
have something made up   i wonder if Pippa will lend
me her long dress   or perhaps a scarf would hide it
i could wear Mummy's opals   or at least the earrings
as if that will make a difference   or my pearls too
i don't want to look showy   Pippa will want to talk
about John Ashton   when   i haven't had a thought

about him   since i met him by chance   well five years
must be ten years ago   or heard of him for so long

Lily
last night when i went out look at the sunset   i saw the
woman goes to a day centre come out   and said what
time is it dear   she thought it was the morning   and
was waiting to be picked up   and she's not that old
i told her   it's a lovely evening dear   it's not the
morning   it's the evening   where's my day gone then
she said   i've got ready   she had her coat on waiting
for them to take her to the day centre   and the sun
going down for her to see   i don't think she's fit to
be on her own poor thing   where's my day gone
where's my day gone   she kept saying   then her
phone rang   and went in and forgot   i was there

Chorus Two

Gita, Sylvia, Marion, Amy, Shirley, Lily

Gita

Laxmi keeps coming into my mind today   and when
she does i think of Grandfather's house then   for she
was the only one left from those times here   the nice
well spoken man who buys his papers from us was in
last night   to buy cigarettes before we closed   said
the sunset in the park   where he had been for a walk
before the evening set in   was just like an African
sunset   you see   and i don't have many memories
of it   for i was so young then   they are just feelings
often sensations   that I try to fill out with   what i
was told   but if i remember i can see Grandfather's
house in the evening   quite clearly still in my mind's
eye   and playing in the courtyard with Sanjit and
Laxmi   the water glittering in the little water ornament
in the centre   and the kala boys doing their work
and the red earth outside   and the big sky   and a big
sun sinking   and Father and Uncle coming back from
business in town   i don't have many other memories
for i was young when we left   the rest of my memories
are always with my mother   always   she said my
father said when we left   remember you were born in
paradise   we never speak Swahili now   only used it
when we didn't want the children to know what we were
saying   Grandfather wouldn't come to England   he
said he was too old   and stayed with his brother
who was some kind of holy man   Grandfather was
very pious by all accounts   poor Laxmi   yes   poor
Laxmi   she was so unhappy in her married life   he
was so spoiled Krishna   so spoiled   and her life a

trial   even after his mother's death   for his sisters
were tyrants   she was never good enough for them
and since her funeral   i've thought about her so much
i have   so at least i was luckier than her   even though
my mother-in-law wasn't as kind as she should have
been   and his sisters spoiled him   the three of them
but i never had the time she had   oh no   Krishna and
she had a business   and indeed when it came to money
they were well off i suppose   but he isn't a nice man to
this day   so full of himself   knowing always what's
best   and his oldest sister trying to rule their lives up
till the end   ooh it's so sad   poor Laxmi   life can be
so sad   life is so sad sometimes

Sylvia
i don't pass muster with her   in the same way i didn't
pass muster with Mummy really   i irritate her in the
same way i think   but then i think very few people do
pass muster with her   but she certainly turned round
things for Jeremy   though he must take some credit for
it   and i am eternally grateful to her for that   but he
certainly has to jump to   and i feel i have to watch my
ps and qs   Ronnie takes absolutely no notice and
grunts but by jove she knows what she wants   she
doesn't think much of me   and she certainly rations
time with the children   and i rather think she'd like to
do without us   but Ronnie's chequebook comes in
handy   and he laughs when i say J's under her thumb
it really irritates me   i suppose it's because she's so
much older than him   and Philippa raises her eyebrow
at the mention of her   she's not Pippa's cup of tea at all
but then we are more conciliatory   up to a point Pippa
says   in the ways she has of being dry   as if i'm not
and i'm as good as gold   i wish he could do more of
his photography   it was the reverse with Mummy and
her mother-in-law   Granny was a respectable old body

and thought Mummy was too smart   too London
and of course in the war when Daddy and Uncle Arthur
were away   she and Mimi had a time of it   both
staying in the house near Granny   and they were
thought not to be quite up to scratch i think   too smart
and Mimi was a bit of scandal   when you think of it
always going up to London   and leaving Pippa with us
and right up until the end   Je Reviens and red nails and
her hair done   to the end   and dining at the Ecu de
France then   Daddy loved Mimi   Grandpa was
certainly was amused by her   but then she was a man's
woman   as Mummy would say   and that's where
Hilda comes in   for her parents were friends of Granny
and Grandpa   and Grandpa and Granny in London
in their little flat in Knightsbridge   were not quite what
Daddy's parents thought was respectable   and quite
hard up in the end   and Grandpa saying i'll have to go
to the Jews   but if I ring Pippa   she'll want to talk
about John   and there's nothing to say   it's thirty
years ago   but she will want to be pumping me about
him

Marion
i used to go with him to a gay bar in the basement under
the carpet shop in the market   run by his cousin Tony
watch yourself hanging round with them   my father
would say   they were in with a south London gang
not his dad   but his uncles certainly were   watch
yourself hang round with them   what's his name was
a connection of theirs   who was killed by them   over
something to do with drugs   he had a big drug
problem himself   and he had AIDS at the end   he
was very violent they say   what's his name again   i
remember going to a funeral with Danny   and it was a
proper villains' do   i never seen so many flowers
and so many flash men   but Danny and his brothers

had nothing to do with all that   only there was a lot of talk about it

Gita

did he get everything at the cash and carry   i left a list of course   why am i worrying   yes i might get a minicab home   it won't cost a lot   i'll be tired   i'm tired now   i'll get a minicab   they'll have a number if not i'll ring the one at home   and what will she make for dinner   yes there   well i must let be i wish i'd asked Sita to come with me   i'm sure she would have   but perhaps if i'm not too tired   we'll go to mandir   i can get some flowers to take from the market here   if i'm home early   and have tea and chat   and have a walk after   if the evening permits   if it's as nice as it promises

Amy

into my dimness   my blueness   and   like the evening when it's peaceful   and everything is blue and soft and still   and i'm in it   as if there was music that i can't hear   it's all so still   and there are trees in the shadows and in the dimness   the softness   in the dark blueness among the shapes i can hear the lady   i can't see her but she's there   everywhere   and i can hear just the sound of her   just softness of saying to me   she's saying   just cooing   as i walk by the trees

Shirley

i was restricted then by what i could approve   with everything questioned and scrutinised   then i used to think that flowers in a jug were an expression of a need to possess   and yet I kept some things in my little room like a secret   but chose like a nun would choose   and like a prisoner hoards   without acknowledging it to myself   but enjoying the exercise of taste   i am pulled back to that now   pulled back now   this pulls me back

Amy

and i walk along a path through the trees   and then a
little way away   through the trees a young lady opens
the door of her chair   and steps out   very light
into the blue softness against   the dark trees   and her
talking to me all the time

Shirley

he was a substitute   the replacement provider of pain
what went on between us a diversion from what should
have been the way forward   a transference   until
rebellion set me free   because i realised at last   at last
i did   that i didn't have to go on with it   and that
i shouldn't go on with it   and it wasn't as it was with
Mum   and self-interest set in   and i did go forward
again   as i couldn't before   and yet it was a station
on the way   as true an expression of my nature   as
could be obtained then   an inevitable   an unsuitable
transference   and his lack of any   interest in me
any ordinariness in the relationship   any everyday
communication   or affection   except basic
communication   and the way he sealed off his life
sealed off his interests   i thought it was a very male
thing   it's alright because i'm doing it   it's alright
because i'm thinking it   i think i thought it was all
implied in his maleness   and that it was a product
of his nature his maleness   and true because of that
and it was   wasn't it an expression of that   it
expressed in a vivid form my adjacence   that it was
active at least   and it acted like a drug   it wasn't even
brutal day to day   except for the punishment   which
i had taken as part of a deal   just cold and indifferent
and the compliance he saught was an exciting   part of
the arrangement   and secret   i blame him only for his
part   and it wasn't that i was seeking small talk   in
its way it was like a marriage based on money   but it's

32

better now in spite of this   but i feel as i walk out   a
lift   a breath   and glad it's over   and remind myself
how much better it is   in spite of things now

Marion

you could walk out of a job in the morning   and get
another in the afternoon   we thought we were so
sophisticated   and yet it was all innocent   when you
think of it   we hardly ever went up the West End
just to the clubs round this way   but we fancied
ourselves for all that   we were mad about clothes and
music   and the boys and their football   but we still
thought then a chara trip to the seaside was a big deal
oh yes

Lily

if i was low this morning   it's because yesterday i got
exhausted shopping   and then i thought   i'd lost my
purse   and was on my way back to the shop   and
found it in my hand   and then when i got home later
i made some supper and put it on a tray   and then it
went flying out of my hand   and broke everything
and   i wept at the clearing up   and i brought both of
them to mind for comfort

Sylvia

when Philippa and i were talking on the phone last night
i asked how long she wore her wedding ring   after she
and Chris divorced   and she said it was quite a
decision   she wore it for months after that   for one
thing she said it had been useful in fending off unwanted
attention   she's just like her mother   anyway eventually
she put it in her jewel case   and then of course it went
in the burglary   i asked because i am able to wear my
wedding ring again   i took it off because my rings were
so loose last year   and i wore it around my neck on a
chain   and then i put it for some reason   in the box

with my marriage lines   and then when i was able to
wear it again now   it was quite a decision   i had
thought i would never take it off   except to put on the
draining board   and then having done it   instead of
putting it on again as a matter of course   i thought
what if what if i don't put it on again   is it too late
just fancy   and then hearing about him dying
thinking   is it really   just a daydream   and guilty
just a proposition one makes   like a cold thought   a
dare   and thinking i wonder what would have
happened   and who would have thought he would
have become a government advisor   one can't stifle
one's thoughts   a foolish wonder

Marion
the families all gone   the sun setting at the end of the
day   the beach deserted except for kids like us still
there   and the tide coming right up   almost against
the promenade wall   and we still in our costumes
the boys diving into the big waves   the waves sucking
up the sand   and mixing with it   the sunset white
and it getting cold   but staying on the beach until it
got too windy   and the evening drawing in   so
nothing for it but to change   holding a towel round
you to dress   and envious of the big bath towels
i had a good figure then   and shake the sand out of
our shoes   and our shoulders and backs burnt from
the sun   even he had sunburnt shoulders   even
though he was so dark   and wring your costume out
and roll it in the towel   and he asked you to put his in
your basket   where was your make-up and purse
and your cardigan   and couple of left sandwiches
and with me always the apple left   and then up to the
funfair   and all the boy so full of themselves   and
daring you to go on the rotor   and the girls screaming
i was quite fearless then   i couldn't now   and bought

34

candyfloss   and rock for the little ones   he won a
little china dog   and gave it to me   but i made him
give it to his mum   you have it   you got to give it to
your mum   you have it   go on   and then if we'd
still got any money   chips   and that was the end of
it then there   all your money gone   so there was
nothing left   for it was time to get on the bus again
and manage a backseat   if you was a lucky   sang If
You Roll a Silver Dollar   and Kay Starr The Wheel of
Fortune   and sleep or cuddle if you was lucky   and
felt him come in the backseat   through his gaberdines

Chorus Three

Gita, Bridget, Sylvia, Lily, Amy, Marion

Bridget
Mary says i should put in for a transfer   it's gone
beyond now   and it was so nice when i first moved
in   there is never a night now without the sirens and
shouting in the street   and last night there was a police
raid in the next block   and it's not long since there was
stabbing there   and they're dealing drugs in the bottom
i'm sure of it   with all the people come in and out
there no doubt in my mind   there's always someone
outside waiting for him   and shouting through the
letter box   and there's always rubbish on the stairs
and the smell in the lift   and it's not good for the
children   all this   where they exchange needles now
across the street from us   and the girl on my landing
she got three dear little kids   it's no place for them
and at least you can see her face   though she's covered
in black   and she has no English to speak of   like all
of them are   it isn't safe for them   and the market is
like the Middle East   whatever that's like   may God
forgive me   Mary won't go there   she remembers it as
a child   and she won't go there now   it's so different
from   there's not a white face on a stall   and all
eating with their hands   and all the women in the
street seem to be covered in black   a different story
than a couple of old rastas playing dominoes on the
green   it's gone right down   it really has   i'd like to
be near Mary   though she said it was always bit rough
round here   still not as bad as this when i first came
here   and i've got a bedroom to offer them

Sylvia (*of the group*)
they could be mother and daughter   the girl doesn't
make the best of herself   she's a respectable little body
strange to be waiting here with these people   and she
seems so too   i never know the religion   for they all
don't cover their heads   but she seems to be a
respectable little body   and she's wearing a cardigan
over it   quite right   she has a baby i think too   i've
seen her with a baby   she must love her baby as much
as another mother   how can it be judged   depends
on the case   her feelings are hers   and as far as one
knows just as deep for the baby as anyone's   but
without knowing what can you think   can she
discriminate   know best for her child   within the
scope of what's on offer   as for refinement   well
discrimination   who knows   does she have the words
that we have   only God knows these things   are our
feelings the same   and what is character after all
well only God knows   she looks as is if she might say
my son the soldier   she looks like a soldier's mother to
me   she looks as if she'd say my son the soldier   she
must have children surely   what do you know of
anybody   does she work   what do they do   is she
on benefits or whatever   i think of Dad's old secretary
Miss Pim   and then i think of what some of them can
get   and   why should someone like her   why
should she be penalised   and sell her house to keep her
old mother   why should she sell her house   that she's
struggled to get   which she might have to do   she's
got a little pension for her father left her something
and Daddy invested it   and they are getting all sorts
are they   what does she keep the baby on   i must go
down and see her at Easter

Lily
i think about him every day   both of them   of course

i do   i think if he'd been there this morning   last
night   when i was so low   he'd have laughed me out
of it   and of course   maybe am i romancing   and
too often thinking of the past   well yes   and i don't
like living in the past   but i miss him   especially now
at this time   when we could be in the garden   with
everything all ready to bloom

Amy
and along the path there are trees again   and through
the trees are princesses   playing in a clearing   and
splashes of gold in the purple behind them   patterns of
gold like splashes   and a border of leaves   and gold
borders   and their dresses are white   and printed
with patterns that i can hardly make out   like flowers
sprinkled over them

Marion
she doesn't want to talk about it   and i have to respect
her privacy   but i don't want her to go through what
i did   and perhaps that's why she won't   and she's
close to her father   which she knows i don't mind
and i am glad   but i don't trust him   he's too pleased
with himself for me   and that wasn't the first time
and I don't like his attitude to her   and i could crown
that girl for telling her she saw him   and she says he
says it wasn't serious   just after she'd had the little one
and three of them to cope with   i have had my share
of it   and i don't want her to go through it   but i'll
have to keep my mouth shut

Lily
my mother kept a garden just big enough to keep some
wallflowers in   at the end of the tiny scrap of yard we
had out the back   next to the lavatory   and where
the copper was   against the whitewashed wall   and
we had a garden from when we was first married

i don't know how i'd do without one now   it's a
blessing   they wouldn't believe it now   how families
managed   in those little houses then   time goes on
i must make sure someone gets my bits and pieces of
china   that come to me from my mother's aunt   who
lived in two rooms not far from us   and she said they
were for me   i remember   she would sit in her chair
with a stiff back   and her dark eyes   and she had
very strong views and church on Sunday   she wanted
me to have schooling   because I was a good reader
and my teacher said she'd put me in for the scholarship
but they couldn't afford it   and took me away   it was
she got me a job in service   with a doctor and his wife
in the village near us   and i didn't like it all   although
she was a nice woman   and it's from her i learned how
to lay a table   and i was always a good needlewoman
so i've been a good housekeeper   i moved to work
in London at the end of the war   and that's where i
met him

Marion
thank God it's different with the other one   and i wish
she lived nearer   anyway i'll see her the weekend
but this one don't know how to look out for herself the
same way   and course she's so pretty   and he's
jealous of her   that's the silly part of it   and i don't
worry the same about Joanne   and he's as good as gold
so be thankful i think   but this one's such a good little
person   she deserves more

Lily
he was the foreman in the next section   he was friend
of my friend Christine's chap   so we got all together
and we loved dancing those days   and i loved the
pictures   we got married when he was on embarkation
leave   before he went abroad   i had a lovely dress
and coat in navy   Dick and Chrissie was our witnesses

we didn't tell anyone else   he didn't meet my mother
till he come back   and we lived first in rooms   and
then in a house   and then in the house down here
and we tried for a baby straight away   but nothing
came to us   until the little one   and he struggled until
he was eighteen months   and then i lost him   and we
didn't have any luck after that   but ooh i was happy
with him   Mrs Hancock admired the china   and i
thought she could have it   but there we are

Sylvia
he expected things of me in a way i had never experienced
before   as if i really had something to say   and why
did Roger go to public school and university   and
not me   and he was amused when i told them about
Mrs Herbert's   and said no wonder   and it's where
Mummy went to school   and i had loved it there
and he demanded things of me   as if he wanted to
rescue me   he drank too much even then   and it
became a problem later on i think   but then it was all
part of the excitement   and he was attractive   and he
dressed well and hid his vanity   and he had style   he
spent most of the time in the West End   in the French
Pub   and the Coach and Horses   and the Bar Italia
and all the rest of it   and they were exciting times for
me   i had had no experience of anything like it   and it
was   i remember it as being rather shocking   and
alive   what's the use of thinking of all that now   he
could never have been faithful   and i was too young to
contemplate that   he married twice   and I shouldn't
think that was all   who would have thought he would
end up being so successful   he was just a would-be
journalist then   and making very little money
spending all his time in Soho pubs   it's not as if i
married to please anyone but myself   it's not as if
i married to please Daddy and Mummy   though

perhaps Ronnie was more like what they were used to
and that must have been in it somewhere   they were
certainly alarmed by John   and it's not as if Daddy
took to Ronnie anyway really   it's not as simple as that
is it   though i think Mummy didn't mind him John
because he was so attractive of course   but i could
never imagine really crossing Daddy   so i feel disloyal
thinking about it at all now

Chorus Four

Shirley, Bridget, Gita, Joy

Shirley
i still wonder what would it be like to dedicate your life
to a man   to find you had the industry to make a home
to have the knack   like a beaver   to live a life
domestic and to the purpose   i think of Dad in good
times   falling asleep in front of the television   and
she waking him with a slap for snoring   and him
laughing   and us laughing   and how happy we could
be   that's what he would have liked it to be always
Dad   but she was so ill   for so much of the time
and she had a deeper understanding   a more profound
compassion than he required   he needed something
more every day   than a sick wife who had in her
something of a deeper intuition   and yet he admired
her   but he wasn't fit for the level of her pain   i think
if I lived my life like that   if i could make more of a
fist of things   i would validate Dad   if i could make
something of life in a pinafore   i would be rewarding
him   that if i could get it right inside me   if i could
get it right inside   it would help him   as if his
reputation is in my hands   that what happened
between them   that how she is   has only made him
look inadequate   if i could lead a celebratory life
like an old railway poster   in a shirt waister   making
malt drinks   in thick bright china   it would create a
world where Dad is always laughing   if i could burn
off the dross   i could make it all right for him

Bridget
i didn't take her home till she was two   they didn't
know about her there before that   and thank God things

have changed there   and haven't they though i
didn't go before because of all that   but then my father
was ill   and they told me I should come home   so
i bucked up the courage   i told my brother Declan
and he told me to bring her   and he was there to meet
me the airport   and said it was no one's business but
mine   and it was fine once i was there   and there was
tears as soon as they saw her of course   and i was glad
to see Dada   but that was the beginning of the end for
him then   as it turned out   so i'm glad   and he died
the next year   and now it's Declan's wedding
anniversary and   oo   I don't know

Shirley
i want to join with other women   i want to coo like
other women   as they   lean over a child   and their
eyes fill with tears   as if this feeling expressed
looking at a baby   cooing its name   and weeping
as if this bliss   this ecstasy   this bliss   this
unbearable joy   as if the tears are payment   that
there must be payment for this happiness   that this
love brings with it feelings like grief   that this bliss
must be paid for

Joy
as if Garry wasn't a worry   now that girl is having a
baby   he's got no sense he thinks i don't know   he's
such a fool   and he hasn't told anyone   but i know
because she told Bernice   and as if he's not got enough
on his plate   he's in enough trouble with his probation
he missed his last appointment   and he can't keep his
mouth shut   when he does go to see the man   and he
won't be told   driving his car like a fool   is what got
him into trouble in the first place   and he can't get
himself out of it   he has to see the man   or they'll
put him away again   oh i miss Dad   i wish he was
here to give us some sense

Shirley

so little of me remains Christian   I wish could face
things with Gran's sweet chapel optimistic certainty of a
possible happy after life   with Christ like the good
breast   instead of picturing all the dead souls in a
diasporic vastness waiting for the end of time   Mum
and Granny pictured eternity as forming around mothers
embracing children   all conflicts resolved in maternal
acceptance   all death a prelude to seeing again a cousin
who you particularly liked   there for you in the
background   death a prelude to aunties greeting you at
the front door   with a kiss and embrace   all
aggression gone   all children climbing on to laps
and kissing and dissolving into holiness for ever

Gita

and worry about Shilpa   for i feel that the way she wants
to live   this way of life what she lives by now   is so
uncertain   and it worries me   i think her ideas are
too easily come by   things are too ready   too quickly
arrived at and solved   too superficial   i agree with
her of course some of the time   about many things i do
and i agree with her of course i do   how wouldn't i
but for all that it's too easy   what she wants there are
some deep things   some bonds that once they are
severed   can't be made up   and worried that she'll be
loose and blown about   losing out of things of the spirit
but she says her life is spiritual   in its own way she
says   is it   and she a serious girl   she is a good girl
she has a good heart   she has   more than me   and
this white boy is a nice boy   i worry of course i do
i think how things have changed   and i envy her
freedom   but i am worried how things have changed

Shirley

i am still in thrall to her unhappiness   in spite of all my
efforts   i am in thrall to her   i can't let it go   i am

44

under a spell   i can't assuage her pain   i have tried to
put a wedge between us   i tried to   but there is no
way out   i felt such pain   her pain all the time
like anyone with an unhappy mother   trying to please
her   and angry with her   but how could she help it
i would look at the tight face   for the smile that was
often there underneath   and the breakthrough of
sunlight   that i knew was there   but i can't assuage
her pain   i felt such pain   her pain all the time
Mother's   my old Mum's pains   and yet i am not
free of her   never will be free   even when she dies
i don't think   i'll be free   i'll ever be free

Chorus Five

Sylvia, Amy, Bridget, Gita, Marion, Joy, Shirley, Lily

Sylvia
i remember at the height of it once he wouldn't let me
leave the sitting room in the flat i shared then with Roger
and putting his back against the door   to prevent my
going   trying to get me to see something he thought it
was vital i understood   trying to alter me fundamentally
in some way   as if he was saving me   and as if it had
to be then   that it couldn't be postponed   that it was
now   that something had to be faced then   and saying
it was all because of Daddy and Mummy   asking me
why i had such a problem with men   saying it was
Mummy and Daddy   that women like me all betrayed
their husbands in their hearts   that i was a coward
incapable of loyalty   and ignorant and prejudiced
and why did i vote as Daddy did   and that anyone
i loved would be subsumed by the family   and all the
good manners were a front   that i was a coward
that it was now   that it had to be now

Amy
i'd go round to Donna's   but it's not fair on her   and
she's been a good friend to me   she has   but it's him
i want   and that's it   only him   i feel so desperate
if he'd just come back and stop this   please   oh please

Bridget
Mary is going to bingo tonight   i'm going to go home
i've a load of washing to do and put it in the machine
the flat's straight   i did that this morning early   and
anyway who's going to see it   and i'm going to get
something i can put into the microwave from Marks

and treat myself   and have a hot bath   with something
nice in it   and wash my hair and put on my nightie
and lie on the sofa under a cover   and watch a film
i haven't watched   the one i got out on Saturday   and
open a bottle of wine   and i'll take something nice for
Yusuf   he likes a doughnut if he comes to see me
and really you can't fault her with the children   you
can't   and he'll toddle along the landing to me if he
hears me in

Sylvia
i was frightened by the strength of his feeling   and in
part excited by it   and frightened   and not knowing
where it would go   and overwhelmed by it   until
then   in the midst of the turbulence   i felt something
inside me through it   my will rising up against his
and then something implacable between us then   that
couldn't move   and yet i felt that   if i had the
wherewithal   something could be made of it   but
then i felt something more ordinary   something of
hang on   something of Daddy   when he had decided
that what was right was right   i was offended by him
expecting me to be subject to his view of things   that i
should be what he thought i should be   it didn't suit
me to be browbeaten   i thought he had a nerve   and
yet in the end it was also because i wasn't romantic
enough to take part in the struggle   to see what would
come to be   i didn't have the nerve   it seemed too
out of the ordinary

Gita
she lives in a lovely little flat   very small   but just
enough space   and easy to keep clean   which her
son bought her on a mortgage   after her husband
died two years ago   she does a couple of hours in the
shop now and then   to help out   and she has the
little ones sometimes   which suits her   and sees her

47

daughter most days   doing well   and a nice good girl
and hasn't she done well   and i worry about Shilpa
then   oh how i envy her the time she has to herself
though i must say it's brave of her   for i couldn't live
now on my own   much as i think of it sometimes
though it's nice now to have the new baby   oh he's a
light in the world   he is   but we're too cramped still

Amy (*to Lily*)
I wish you was my nan

Sylvia
and I had the most awful dream about Mummy the
other night   why was that   i can't remember   it
was an awful dream about Mummy

Marion (*to Amy*)
Tina? Is that you, Tina?

Amy
Yes.

Marion
You alright?

Bridget
i'll be glad to get hom.

Joy (*to Gita*)
Why are you doing this?

Gita (*to Joy*)
What? What am I doing?

Joy
You know what you're doing.

Gita
I don't, now leave me alone.

Joy
You have to.

Gita
You get on with your life and leave me alone. We'll be alright.

Joy
You see.

Gita
What do I see? What do I see?

Sylvia
What foolish thoughts you have.

Marion (*to Amy*)
What is it?

Amy
Nothing.

Marion
Tell me.

Amy
No.

Marion
Tell me.

Amy
It's nothing.

Marion
What's the matter? Tell me. What's the matter with you?

Amy
Nothing's the matter.

Marion
Tell me.

Amy
It's nothing, Mum. Now leave it, will you.

Lily
I thought she could have them. They'll have to go to someone.

Shirley
Mummy.

Sylvia
Well, if I didn't tell you, who would?

Shirley
Really.

Sylvia
It's all very well.

Shirley
Really, Mummy.

Marion
he wanted to be young for ever   he felt trapped   all the rest of it   people move on and all that   and in the

end what he left for   it didn't last   and he's still on
his own   acting the fool   but i don't think men can
be faithful in the same way   it's not really in their
nature is it   so when Tina said about the man moved
in next door but one   i had already thought of it
and he seems a nice fellow   but i couldn't go through
all that again   better as it is   i have had a few
romances since   but that's it for me i think   and i've
got used to being single now   i couldn't go through all
the nonsense with him again   all the heartache
i thought i would die then   i felt so hopeless   but
i didn't have any of what I think she's gone through
it was only the once   the one time and finished for me
nothing when we were young   like that   and i don't
trust him   whatever she says   but it's not my business
is it   and whatever i say she has to lead her own life

Gita (*to Shirley*)
Why don't you come home?

Shirley
I don't want to come home.

Bridget (*to Amy*)
Leave him with me. I'll have him. You can leave him
with me.

Gita (*to Shirley*)
What kind of a life is this you're leading?

Shirley (*to Gita*)
My life.

Sylvia
his mother was a comforting little body

Amy (*to Bridget*)
Will you, just for an hour?

Bridget (*to Amy*)
Yes, you go on, go, I'll have him.

Sylvia
i met him through a girl I was at secretarial college with
her brother was at university with him

Lily
i'll be glad to get home

Sylvia
he lives in South Africa now

Gita
i envy the two sisters who come into the shop sometimes
for something   who seem so self-sufficient   little
respectable English ladies   very nicely dressed   and
their hair always seeming to be just done at the
hairdresser's   and always smiling   and they go to
church   and one of them smokes   the younger one
i think   if i could have company like that maybe
i envy her in her little flat   but i don't think i could
manage like that   on my own i would be lost   oh this
envy   it's so wrong   so bad so bad   when i am a
lucky woman   if you think of it

Sylvia
i suppose I wanted a conventional life   it was too rich
for me   what he wanted   it was too intense   in
spite of the excitement   and the fun of it   it was too

romantic   it didn't really suit me   i was   i am too
coarse-grained perhaps   even now i see things that are
disconcerting   things in the newspapers   and think
oh well 'twas ever   and that acts like a blanket over it

Shirley (*of Sylvia*)
does she have a cleaner   i bet she has she looks as if
she has servants   does she have a treasure   she
certainly does

Sylvia
i wonder if Hilda will want to go to a concert   she
usually does when she's in town

Shirley (*of Sylvia*)
she's the kind of woman Mum would have addressed as
Mrs so-and-so   in a particular way to combine the
deference coming from admiration   while retaining a
sense of herself   they collude women like that
Mummy and she   she would have called Mum missus
out of respect   and in a tone that kept up the
difference all the same   so they knew where they were

Sylvia
and much talk of RVW there   and in other respects
ordinary as ordinary   but music was all for them
Mummy said

Lily
i'm just an old lady at the bus stop it must seem   when
you're old you change your status in the world   i'm
just an old dear to say hello to now

Sylvia
they harboured a very eminent German Jewish man in
the war who was very much a figure in it all then

Marion
and John's the same

53

Bridget
i don't want to feel so lonely

Sylvia
and he seemed to show no gratitude at all she said

Lily
who will close your eyes   who will see you buried
you never thought of these things   nothing prepares us

Shirley (*to Sylvia*)
Why whatever it is I say, Mummy, do you do this?

Sylvia
What do I do?

Shirley
You always do it.

Sylvia
Oh really? What do I do? I've just been saying what I
thought.

Shirley
You do it every time I express an opinion, Mummy. You
do. Whenever I say anything. You do.

Sylvia
What do you mean? You do talk such nonsense,
Catherine. There is always another way of looking at
things you know, only you don't seem to think so.

Shirley
But you aren't saying that because there is another way
of looking at things, that's not why.

Sylvia
You are so hectoring always, you are so certain, as if
there wasn't another point of view. You're such a tyrant

the way you go on about things, so certain you're right about things, and I won't be bullied by you.

Shirley
It's you, it's you.

Sylvia
Oh really.

Shirley
You do.

Sylvia
Oh I don't give a toss, say what you like, say what you like, say what you like.

Lily
Shall we go into M and S and have a cup of tea? Is that what you'd like?

Gita
Yes, it is, it is.

Lily
Let's go there then.

Joy (*to Marion*)
I can't put up with this any more. I can't do it. I can't do it. I won't.

Marion (*to Amy*)
You want to look after yourself now. You want to take hold. You want to forget him now.

Bridget
And then there's this wedding anniversary.

Shirley
like a wall between me and Daddy and the world

Lily
i can't manage it all on my own

Joy
i got ice cream for them after

Amy
and the baby on the ground in the light under the tree
and her voice is so sweet

Joy
i don't know where my money goes

Shirley
and i felt the disapproval of her not being able to snap
out of it   as they thought she could

Sylvia
and there's a big difference between Hilda's taste in
music and her taste in everything else

Shirley
all of them

Sylvia
i'll go and see Roger later?

Joy
i worry he is growing to be like Garry   he looks like
him   and he's too good-looking for his own good
like him   and   he'll never grow up   and he wants
to be mister man   the way he talks   and all the big
ideas   and it won't get him anywhere   but there's no
getting him to see sense   no talking to him

Sylvia
i told him   you will end up with an old drunk on your
hands   and then where will you be   that will be too

awful   and you'll feel bad then having to get rid of him
then   if you leave it   best deal with it now

Lily
no one left   no one who knew you when you were
young   for a long time now

Sylvia
he was left money by an old friend   and it's enough for
him to buy something of his own

Gita
i'll get red flowers

Sylvia
and it worries me

Marion
i'll have him tomorrow and Shelby the weekend

Sylvia
they came over from Australia together

Bridget
and when i finally got through the water people   they
said they think there must be a leak

Marion
why do you put up with it i said

Bridget
you get the first call-out free so that's lucky

Amy
blue blue

Sylvia
i wonder what she'll wear today

Shirley
i've been good because I was afraid of being bad

Joy
he's good in the kitchen   like Dad

Lily
yes yes

Shirley
why does God require the constant recrucifixion of his
son when we have prevented unknown catastrophes
which he denies all knowledge of

Bridget
and so much concern they had for the poor   and so
much of what it believes   is tied up so much with the
poor

Shirley
making the eternal present in the sky

Bridget
and yet it goes on   the poor goes on   and nothing
done about it but praying and collecting   and it's
God's will

Sylvia
and Jeremy   thank God thank God

Shirley
see other people by the spill of my own concern for
myself

Lily
and wonder when there will be nothing else   no energy
for anything else?

Shirley
object is subject to itself

The next five lines overlap.

Lily
mustn't dwell

58

Shirley
now is eternal

Amy
says I am better off

Shirley
the dead do not sing

Lily
you wonder that you ever could?

Shirley
if our saviour could not   how will this worry

Sylvia (*of Shirley*)
she could make more of herself

Shirley
i was bound by the horizon never looking up and seldom
from side to side

Joy
let him go

Sylvia (*of Shirley*)
like Jane Eyre

Bridget
i hope it doesn't get cold

Joy
perhaps it will turn out to be something

Amy
hold him up in my arms

Joy
you never know

Shirley
i have crossed a line invisible to the people

Marion
living his life as if he wasn't married   like he was single

Lily
no one   no one at all?

Joy
if it went well tonight

Marion
my nan told me her mother came to this country from
Russia when she was fourteen she came here alone with
nobody and nothing except for some money stitched
into her petticoat

Amy
and look out of the window into the dark

Lily
holding them against her cheek to see if they were aired

Shirley
this struggle for goodness

Marion
a betting gang my father said

Joy
Garry said he looks like Dad   and she was furious
and saying he's nothing like him

Amy
it's all i can do

Shirley
i am unknown to love?

Lily
i want to go home

Sylvia
would i leave him

Lily
we could be waiting to be shipped out   we could be
waiting for   are we waiting you might ask

Gita
why do i do it   why do i think it?

Joy
how long is this   going to be

Bridget
still the feeling walking past

Marion
people move on he said

Bridget
oh she was a villain she was   oh don't bear to think
about

Shirley
i told myself that if you did a good action something
good would come out of it

Amy
i'll go home and make him his tea and put him to bed
and then when it's getting dark i'll pick him up and hold
him close and look out of the window

Lily
i remember waiting for the results   waiting and waiting

Joy
the lady said it could be anything

Marion
are you sitting down   i said no   she said you better
sit down   i got a bit of bad news for you   there's
been a letter   i opened it   so I sat down on a pair of
packing boxes which was near the phone where i was in
work

Shirley
as if there can be no more beautiful days

Gita
she'll make something   i won't worry

Bridget
and for all her good intentions she was a villain   she
was   she was trapped   that's what it was

Sylvia
and thinking about him now

Marion
i thought i'd moved on   people move on he said
well look at him now   well and i have moved on
but you still feel it   i thought I wouldn't cope
couldn't   but i did cope   i thought I would die then

Amy
i'll hold the baby close and look out of the window

Lily
he was my dear

Marion
the things you feel

Bridget
i'll see them the weekend   and then I can pet the baby
and i'll go up there Easter perhaps   we'll see

Shirley
when i've set fire to myself in a park   set fire to myself
in some newspaper park   when i've poured it over me
the petrol then when flames   whoosh like wind across
the trees   then   when you've imprisoned me   after
my hands have gone up against the butts   or perhaps
have gone up after the door has burst open against the

62

bullets   or when i am in a ward   starving   in a
hospital   where i am lying

Sylvia
could i do without him

Shirley
most of my life was foreign to me as it was presented
most of life as it was presented   was alien to me

Bridget
oh the bloom on him

Amy
i wish you was my nan

Shirley
being loved I suppose brings its own labour

Joy
as if   i would

Bridget
oh the hypocrisy

Shirley
even a crown won't prevent worry

Bridget
they lost their first   grandchild   when it was an
infant   poor child   which made her despair then
for until that time she had believed faithfully in
everything she had been taught   while the tragedies of
other people   had passed her by   in her general
compassion   and God's will   and the rest of it   but
then as time went on   and as she lived life as it came
again   thoughts of the dead child   did not come so
often   and belief came to her as easy as it had been

Lily
i hope it's not going to get cold

Sylvia
thank God thank God

Amy
please please

Gita
and say my prayers